Almost Love

Poems of Unsaid Affection, Fleeting
Connections, and Love's Lingering Absence

Nuzhat Ismail

BookLeaf
Publishing

India | USA | UK

Made with ❤ on the BookLeaf Publishing Platform
www.bookleafpub.in
www.bookleafpub.com

Dedication

To the hearts that have loved, both in silence and in word. This collection is for those who have known the sweetness of affection unspoken, whether in romance, friendship, or family. For the friendships that carried unvoiced longing, for the love between parents and children that was never fully expressed, and for the romantic "almosts" that linger in memory—this book is for you.

To my own heart, which has known both the joy and the ache of what was never fully spoken—thank you for allowing me to explore and express these quiet, unspoken feelings. These words are for all the unspoken love we carry.

Preface

Almost Love is a collection that seeks to capture more than just the fleeting moments of romantic attraction. While it delves deeply into the sweet, uncertain stages of falling for someone and the lingering ache of unrequited love, it also reflects on the unspoken connections that exist in the other significant relationships of our lives—whether with friends, family, or even with ourselves.

In these poems, I explore the quiet spaces between people—the moments where love and care are felt but never expressed, where understanding lingers without ever being voiced. Sometimes love is felt in a fleeting glance, a gesture, or a silence that speaks louder than words. The poems in this collection reflect not just the romantic "almost" love that never fully materialized, but also the unacknowledged feelings in friendships, relationships with parents, and the complexities of love that remains untold.

If you have ever longed for someone's love—whether romantic or not—and felt the weight of what could have been but was never spoken, these poems are for you. They are a reflection of the quiet yearning that we all experience, in many forms, over the course of our lives.

Acknowledgements

Writing **Almost Love** has been a journey of reflection, discovery, and an exploration of the many ways love manifests in different relationships and situationships. I would like to extend my heartfelt thanks to those who have supported me throughout this process.

To my family and friends—your unwavering belief in me, your encouragement, and your patience have been my anchors.
A special mention to my brother **Musaddiq**—your constant support and belief in my ideas have meant more to me than words can say.

I would also like to express my deep gratitude to Book Leaf Publishing for believing in my work and providing the platform to share these poems with the world.

To my readers—thank you for your willingness to journey with me through the ambiguous and bittersweet spaces of love.

And finally, to my own heart—thank you for not giving up on love even when some of it was never truly mine to keep.

1. Say my name

Stars appear brighter,
Blossoms have a deeper hue
I can't help but wonder,
as l walk 'The walk of shame'
What makes me blush,
is not your touch
It's the way you take my name

2. Rendezvous

And when I saw your beautiful face again I could swear
it was more beautiful than all;
all the versions of it I had saved in the recesses of my
brain
You have more of grey now, but this grey I love
It's not the colour of ambiguity or secrets anymore, not
of the 'in-betweens' These strands are testament to how
this, what we have, has stood the test of time And your
eyes, deeper than before, can still hold all of my soul and
heart in them, capable of igniting, inciting and inviting
Your hands still as soft, yet that grip so firm
Your lips... those soft lips that I want to hold between
mine; when I do, it's like putting everything else around
us, to a pause, even if momentarily
And in those brief moments, you, that version of you and
all its shades, all its flaws are mine; blurring the lines
between delusion and reality
It is both beautiful and ironic that I can love you from
afar and you have no say in it; not because I'm
indifferent, but because I'm not

You can give all of you to another and I will still own
what I have with you; for it is mine, in every you and in
every rendezvous!

3. Death of a lover

Only the ones who've tasted it, can tell what it's like...
Alas, they don't live to tell
I've always thought of death as painful,
not so much for the dying but for the ones around
But to find pleasure in a loved one's death, isn't a
common sound
What many don't know of, is the relief it can bring
When you stop waiting for messages or for your phone
to ring
It's easier to let go when they're not coming back
You go easy on yourself, cut some slack
And for these reasons and more, I lied
Told myself that you and all versions I loved, had, a slow
death died
I'd been mourning for months anyway,
but today I wore that new black outfit and inconsolably
cried
Has the beloved died or the lover in me?
Poetry often brings such mystery

"Go deeper", I say, with the same pleasure
As I bury you away, like an unwanted treasure
And what if I see you in flesh someday...
I've been deluded for months, what's with one day!

4. Happy Birthday!

Ah! The delusion; that not speaking to you, not seeing
you will make me forget you
But we've been there before, more times than I
remember today
"Out of sight, out of mind", said whoever, perhaps, didn't
love as much
Or didn't know how the heart only yearns more as days
go by
Love, an addiction, makes you want that which is not
good for you, sometimes
But then what's to say you were not good for me, that I
couldn't have been worse off?
And it's questions this sort, I have learned to suppress in
a quarry
But, even silenced, they lay there and I deceive myself
That a vacation may take my mind off you
That if I had a travel itinerary, perhaps I'd forget your
birthday
That I would be petty to not wish you if you didn't wish
me on mine

But I remember it, all of that week, before and after it
The dilemma and contemplation
Of being petty or the bigger person
Of incommunicado or established contact
And I'm not sure if I am disappointed or pleased by these
notions
Perhaps, the uncertainty is both my fear and addiction
Not knowing when we could stop talking but knowing
you would come back, or not; even if you say you never
left..
Happy Birthday!

5. Missing You...

I miss you, in ways you can't fathom
In ways I cannot explain
In ways that words will only circle the drain
Some days I think, what is there to miss
For I should have forgotten your touch and kiss
If it was your face, I have a picture too many
For your voice, I could pick from saved notes,any
Then I remember, what its like to have you around
Missing something, lost, then found
To be lost again, then found someday
Destiny's hide and seek at play
I miss being both; a child and a woman
Being curious, captivated by only one
I miss laughing at your typos, being careful with mine
Telling you what sucks and what is going fine
Like I drug, I try to quit you and keep failing
For I succumb to the pleas of my heart ailing
Fill the void in my flesh and soul,
Heal my heart and make me whole
Or leave, I beg, and never return

And we can both be forever, forlorn and; burn.

6. Crumbs

And then you appeared, out of nowhere
Admitting you miss me, showing you care
And I believe you only because it's easier on my heart
than to remember the pain, that tore me apart
You ask me of my whereabouts and I bare it all
l ask you if you missed me, why didn't you call?
You brush it off effortlessly in your style
And say that my question made me sound vile
"I want to hear you, I miss your voice..."
"Could you call me once, if that's my choice?"
And I'm still waiting for my phone to ring
Like this, I've spent many an evening
That turned to nights dark, and mornings bright
And once again, you were nowhere in sight
I know better than to sit and wait; but
Like a lioness for its prey, I salivate
Cos you've thrown me crumbs, to watch me drool
But you satiate your hunger, make me a fool
I no longer remember; what it's like to crave
My love for you, I might take to the grave

But that bread and bed are now both rotten
And you're best as the lover that I have forgotten

11

7. Just Like That

And just like that, I stopped checking...
Checking up on you, my messages if you'd read
Checking if you'd responded to anything I'd said
Checking if you'd come back; hoping for you to
Checking if you missed me; wishing you could kiss me
too
Checking all the pictures; memories I wanted to keep
What was; thinking what could be; crying myself to
sleep
And just like that, someday, you'll stop being my muse
But I'll write of your roses and not of your ruse

8. A Letter to my bestie...

"Why write me a letter?", you'd perhaps ask
Cos saying it out loud can be quite a task
I know I haven't been the same 'me' in the recent past
And I've been hoping for this phase to not last
I've stopped questioning myself and pondering on the
reason
I think I must wait it out like a season
But this letter is to tell you something you probably
know
Even when I explicitly don't state so
You're important to me, and anything but forgotten
To my humid summer, you're the calming cotton
I think of you, more often than you perceive
Not just when I have to laugh or grieve
Too often, I pick the phone to make that call
But then I wonder, "what will I talk about, after all?"
No pleasantries, no updates, I have nothing to say
I don't feel it in me to ask you about your day
Not that my cup is too empty to pour into yours

And my heart hasn't yet, shut its doors
Should you need me, I am always here
To hold you, to laugh, to shed a tear
So, I go on with my day, hoping yours was fine too
Praying that when I'm back to myself, I'd still have you

9. To my first love - Dad

I want to run my hands through your hair; sit by your
side
Perhaps let out the love l've been struggling to hide
But I'm scared of letting down my guard; you know
Of telling you I love you, that I don't want you to go
That I may've despised you in moments but l've always
loved you more
Your child; I'm all you from surface to core
That I need you to get better; that we need more time
To laugh at immoral jokes, argue over news and crime
That I'll bring you all you like, if you'd only eat
That a man of your stature cannot accept defeat
That every drop in your weight makes my heart sink
That it's inevitable, of what I must not think
Yet, here I am... lying away
For it will break us both if we were to say
Of our love to each other, hidden in recesses deep
So, cowardly, I continue to weep, this strong facade I
continue to keep
Until the day I've enough armour

To confess that I love you father

10. Allergic and Anxious

An allergy I had, to peanuts, I found
How could that happen?
Couldn't wrap my head around
The slightest trace could make me vomit
I'd request all chefs to kindly omit
This ingredient, monstrous, a threat to my life
Asked friends to check every spoon and knife
Mere possibility of one would make me nauseous
Purposeful consumption, a suicide, obvious
Yet there lay, in a pool of puke
For I stayed away, but it found me by fluke
Uncalled for, it came, | could've eaten better
Scanning every ingredient, letter by letter
I lay there helpless, hoping for the seizures to stop
For some comfort, a pill to pop
For it just needs a trigger, one of any kind
Allergy is to the body, what anxiety is to the mind
Uninvited the same, life threatening indeed
One could only be so careful of the thoughts they feed
One tiny trigger, just one thought

And there it is, the infamous knot
There, they lie, helpless, hoping for the palpitations to
stop
For some comfort, perhaps, a pill to pop
Ignorant of one; of the other, well, aware
Look for signs, if you choose to care
Peanuts, people or a memory canned
Don't judge the cause, just understand!

11. I missed you, may be...

In the misheard lyrics of a song
And the silence that sang along
Just maybe, I missed you.
In conversations filled with intended pun
And the accompanying isolation
Just maybe, I missed you.
On nights starry, quiet and dark
And fights that didn't quite meet the mark
Just maybe, I missed you.
On dates that I'd rather have missed
And sips of coffee my lips kissed
Just maybe, I missed you.
Someday this lite when you're by my side
And when again I will begin to confide
I'll hold you close my friend and kiss you
And tell you maybe, just how much I missed you.

12. The Black Hole

Perhaps, there was something between them
Wrapped safely under the blanket of feigned ignorance
Tucked under the pillow of reluctant acceptance
A spark that shouldn't have caught fire
Words that shouldn't have escaped the barricades of
their parched lips
A lava of emotions desirous to break the constraint of
denial
But volcanoes erupt and stars collide
And sometimes you're left with a black hole

13. The Knot In My Stomach

I have this knot in my stomach that doesn't seem to
untie
tied to a bag so anxiously, with a million reasons why
I have this knot in my stomach the place where
insecurities lie
the home for all those butterflies when I'm sad or high
I have this knot in my stomach from experiences over
years
this knot that just gets tighter with all my childish fears
I have this knot in my stomach, they say it's in my head
have they not seen the demons that hide under my bed?
I have this knot in my stomach from people who've
walked away
from the ones who didn't look back and the ones who
couldn't stay
I have this knot in my stomach it makes me uneasy, I cry
this knot that doesn't loosen up, no matter what I try
I know this knot in my stomach the day I can untie
Out will fly the demons and I'll be soaring high

14. Spring

And then he asked me one day...
"What is your favourite time of the year?"
"Spring", I said
"The season that reminds barren trees of their purpose
and potential.
The time of the year that proves that serenity succeeds
chaos, if only one was patient.
That, by sheer design, leaves have to fall once they're not
strong enough and it is okay for that to happen.
The first bloom being the reminder that sometimes death
is important for a new life, even if detachment may seem
life threatening in the moment.
The time of the year that brings joy, hope and love by its
sheer presence.
And you..."
"Me??", he asked
"Yes, you", I said.
"You're the spring to my autumn!"

15. The Rose

Hidden away, perhaps treasured
Caressed by his fingertips, for times measured
Is this what I will always be?
In a book, his favourite, but, for none to see...

16. Last (but not last) touch

Are we parting ways?
I feel the cheer disappearing from my days
And I know friends can get distant too
but what do you do, when some one means the world to
you?
I AM losing you, wish t'was a lie
Just hug me once, let me cry
I can only hope, I'm not asking for much
A kiss on your forehead, one last touch?
Let me love you while I can
For, like you, I shall love no other man

17. Sand

"What was he like?"
"Sand", I say.
"Fine, grounded
Coarse, grainy, well-rounded
Warm enough to soak in
Cold, yet comforting to bare my soul
To the roaring sea within me, often the shore.
But do you know what they say about sand?"
"What", she asked.
"Hold it too tight, hold it too loose and it slips from your
hand."

18. The Dainty Exhibit

I put all of its beauty out on a tray
Laced with beauty and artistry at play
For someone to behold and admire the real
In colours to many - gold, scarlet, teal
You walked past by and smiled at me
looking at the tray appreciatively
You saw the intensity, the undying flare
My beauty, vulnerability, lying bare
You held it in your eyes, as though you'd known
The fabric, the tapestry, as your very own
Hope tapped by shoulder with a gentle ray
You looked deep in my eyes, then looked away
I gripped my fabric, in a tight clutch
for many, I know, it has been 'too much'
And even with all resilience and soul
It's missing parts, seemingly not whole
Takers, it might not find, after all ; I admit
So I walk away, wrapping my dainty exhibit

19. Bury Yourself

Bury yourself in work, they said
Don't let your mind go astray
Don't worry about the future, don't dwell on the past
Live your life for the day
Don't give your mind no time to think
Don't let your heart, for a moment,sink
You will be fine only if you tried
You will be fine, if you abide
They said, I tried
Yet I cried cos here's what they did not say
Like a tide you'll have highs and lows
Some with bliss; some dismay
Work may keep you busy but when you hit your bed at
night
You'll miss them and how, their voice, their touch and
long for a sight
You'll break, you'll burn
You'll toss and turn no matter what pill you take
And you'll long for their hug in those dark hours as the
only cure to your ache

Tired, some moment, you'll drift to sleep for some
needed rest
And wake up next morning, all set for another resilience
test
And there'll be a time, a moment someday; all this you'll
not feel
Then would you say you're thick skinned now or have
you begun to heal?

20. Gone too soon

As I walk past the graves of the many who've gone
Leaving behind numerous, gloomy and forlorn
At 70, 60 or 45, how soon is 'too soon' for a loved one to
die?
When one hasn't seen enough, or seen it all?
Is one ever 'prepared' to answer this call?
Like autumn befalling a tree leaved,
Death makes them bare and empty, hearts bereaved
Inevitable it is, so we're taught; yet left so befuddled and
distraught
But an autumn harsh holds the promise of a spring
To recompense the loss of life, what could one possibly
bring?
We grieve, we believe, oh the thoughts we conceive!
'twas perhaps for the best, ourselves, we attempt to
deceive
Like the space left by a book, on a library shelf
Living one day at a time, having lost a part of ourself
And then comes an unexpected downpour on a lazy
afternoon,

a picture, a song ... the memory of a loved one gone too
soon!

21. Answer me!

Why is our story darker than this night?
How did we give up? why did we not fight?
Do I cross your mind, do you think of me?
Do you miss my scent, miss what we could be?
Do you feel this painful void in your chest?
Then do you console yourself that it was for the best?
Do your eyes well up with tears when you think how we
broke what could stay for years?
Then how do you get yourself to sleep when all you
want
to do is sulk and weep?
Answers to these questions, tell me, where do you keep?
Tell me, oh friend, what do you do
When you lose someone you love as much as I loved
you?